AF433696

To all the little boys in the world,

This book is dedicated to you, adventurous souls with hearts full of wonder. May these pages be a gateway to endless adventures and discoveries. Remember, this is just the beginning of our journey together. More stories await, more mysteries to unravel. Join us as we explore the wonders of the world one book at a time.

With love and excitement,

DAIAN BOOKS

Once upon a time, in a picturesque town nestled among rolling hills, there lived a curious boy named Sebastian.

Sebastian was always fascinated
by the wonders of nature.

But one day, while wandering near the edge of the forest with his faithful companion Leo, he heard something peculiar.

It was the sound of whispers, soft and gentle, but unmistakably coming from the trees themselves.

Intrigued by the mysterious voices, Sebastian followed them deeper into the forest, with Leo trotting faithfully at his side.

As they walked deeper, they
stumbled upon a small clearing
where the trees seemed to gather,
their branches forming a natural
canopy above their heads.

Strange symbols adorned the bark
of the trees, and in the center of
the clearing lay a piece of
parchment, upon which cryptic
markings glowed faintly.

Determined to unravel the mystery of the talking trees, Sebastian and Leo set out on a search through the enchanted forest.

Along the way, they encountered peculiar woodland creatures eager to help, from mischievous squirrels to wise old owls.

Guided by cryptic clues and riddles, they ventured deeper into the heart of the forest, where the secret of the talking trees awaited them.

Finally, Sebastian and Leo reached the heart of the forest, where they found an ancient and majestic tree like they had never seen before.

As they approached, the tree began to speak, its voice deep and resonant, echoing through the forest.

He revealed to them the secret of
the talking trees: that each tree
had a spirit, a soul and a story to
tell.

And listening with an open heart,
one could hear the trees
whispering, sharing their wisdom and
their love for the natural world.

With the mystery solved and the secrets of the forest revealed, Sebastian and Leo said goodbye to their new friends and began their journey back to the town.

Along the way, they reflected on the lessons learned: the importance of listening, respecting nature, and appreciating the wonders of the world around them.

And upon returning home, they carried with them not only memories of their adventure, but also a new sense of wonder and appreciation for the beauty of the natural world.

And so, dear reader, Sebastian and
Leo's adventure came to an end,
but their journey was just
beginning.

Because from that day on, they would always remember the secret of the talking trees and the valuable lessons they had learned.

And as they looked up at the rustling leaves and dancing branches, they knew that the magic of the forest would live forever in their hearts.

The end.

www.ingramcontent.com/pod-product-compliance
Lightning Source LLC
Chambersburg PA
CBHW060620120726
48002CB00010B/3052